PLANT LIFE CYCLES

JOSEPH MIDTHUN   SAMUEL HITI

BUILDING BLOCKS

SCIENCE

WORLD BOOK

www.worldbook.com

World Book, Inc.
180 North LaSalle Street
Suite 900
Chicago, Illinois 60601
USA

For information about other World Book publications,
visit our website at www.worldbook.com
or call 1-800-WORLDBK (967-5325).
For information about sales to schools and libraries,
call 1-800-975-3250 (United States),
or 1-800-837-5365 (Canada).

Building Blocks of Science:
  Plant Life Cycles
ISBN: 978-0-7166-7881-6 (trade, hc.)
ISBN: 978-0-7166-7889-2 (pbk.)
ISBN: 978-0-7166-2964-1 (e-book, EPUB3)

Acknowledgments:
Created by Samuel Hiti and Joseph Midthun
Art by Samuel Hiti
Text by Joseph Midthun
Special thanks to Syril McNally

TABLE OF CONTENTS

Plant Life Cycles.................................... 4

Reproduction 6

Flowers 8

Cross-Pollination..................................10

Fruits... 12

Conifers 14

The Traveling Seed 16

Germination.. 18

Asexual Reproduction 20

Seedless Plants 22

Growth in Different Climates...............24

Life Cycle Disruptions 26

A Web of Cycles...................................28

Glossary.. 30

Find Out More...................................... 31

Index 32

There is a glossary on page 30. Terms defined in the glossary
are in type **that looks like this** on their first appearance.

PLANT LIFE CYCLES

At first glance, this little plant seed looks about as lively as a pebble.

But, seeds are actually living things.

Within its hard protective layer is a tiny plant waiting to grow.

When the seed is triggered to grow, it can sprout and produce a young, or immature, plant called a **seedling.**

If the seedling survives, it can grow to adulthood and form a mature plant, such as a tree.

POP

All living things go through different stages as they grow and develop.

These stages make up the **life cycle.**

Life cycles help us understand how living things change over time.

Unlike animals, plants do not move from one place to another.

They live through an entire life cycle in one place.

Plants mix carbon dioxide, a gas in the atmosphere, with water and sunlight to make energy through a process called **photosynthesis.**

You use this energy when you eat plants as food.

Plants give off oxygen during photosynthesis. Without this gas, you would experience a life cycle disruption.

So, you might say, it's in your best interest to learn as much about plants as humanly possible!

Your cells would die.

The stages through which any **organism** passes during its lifetime is called its life cycle.

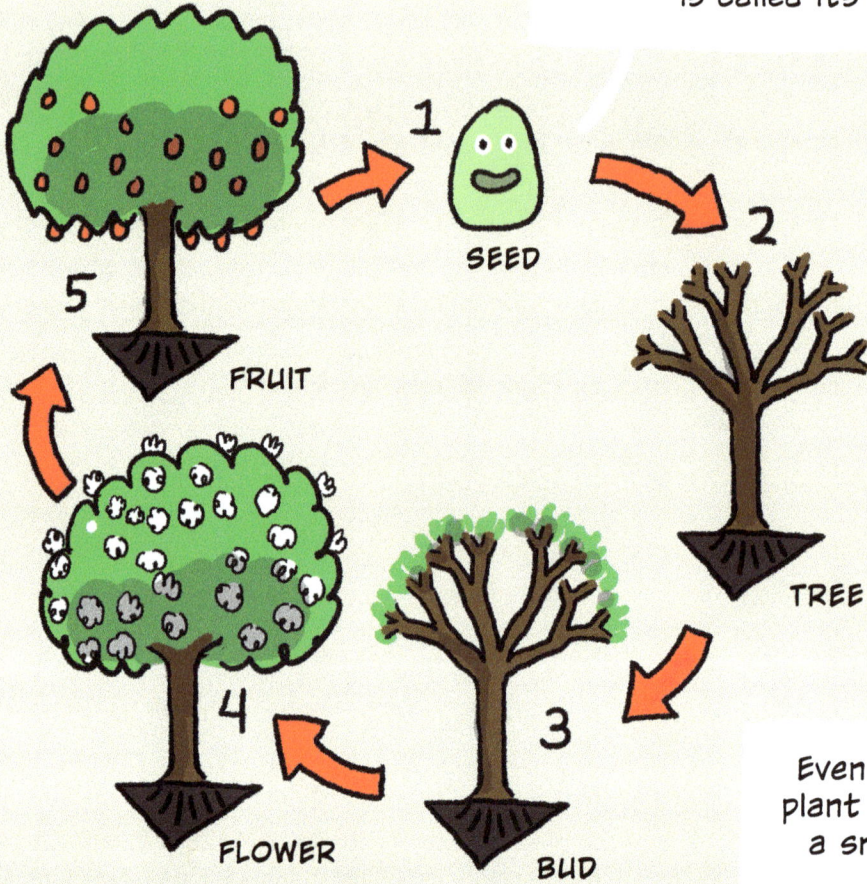

1 SEED

2

TREE

3 BUD

4 FLOWER

5 FRUIT

Every new life cycle begins with **reproduction.**

Reproduction is the creation of **offspring.**

Even the largest plant began life as a smaller seed.

And a mature plant can make new seeds—

Plop

—beginning the next life cycle.

POP.

Every kind of living thing reproduces.

Without reproduction, organisms would die off completely.

Sexual reproduction is common in the animal kingdom, but it is also found in the plant kingdom.

Sexual reproduction involves cells from two parents.

In the animal kingdom, this means a mother and a father.

But a single plant can have both female and male—mother and father—parts.

Most seed plants make flowers.

The male and female parts of some plants are found inside a structure called a flower.

They are called flowering plants, or **angiosperms.**

This flower has the ability to be both mother and father.

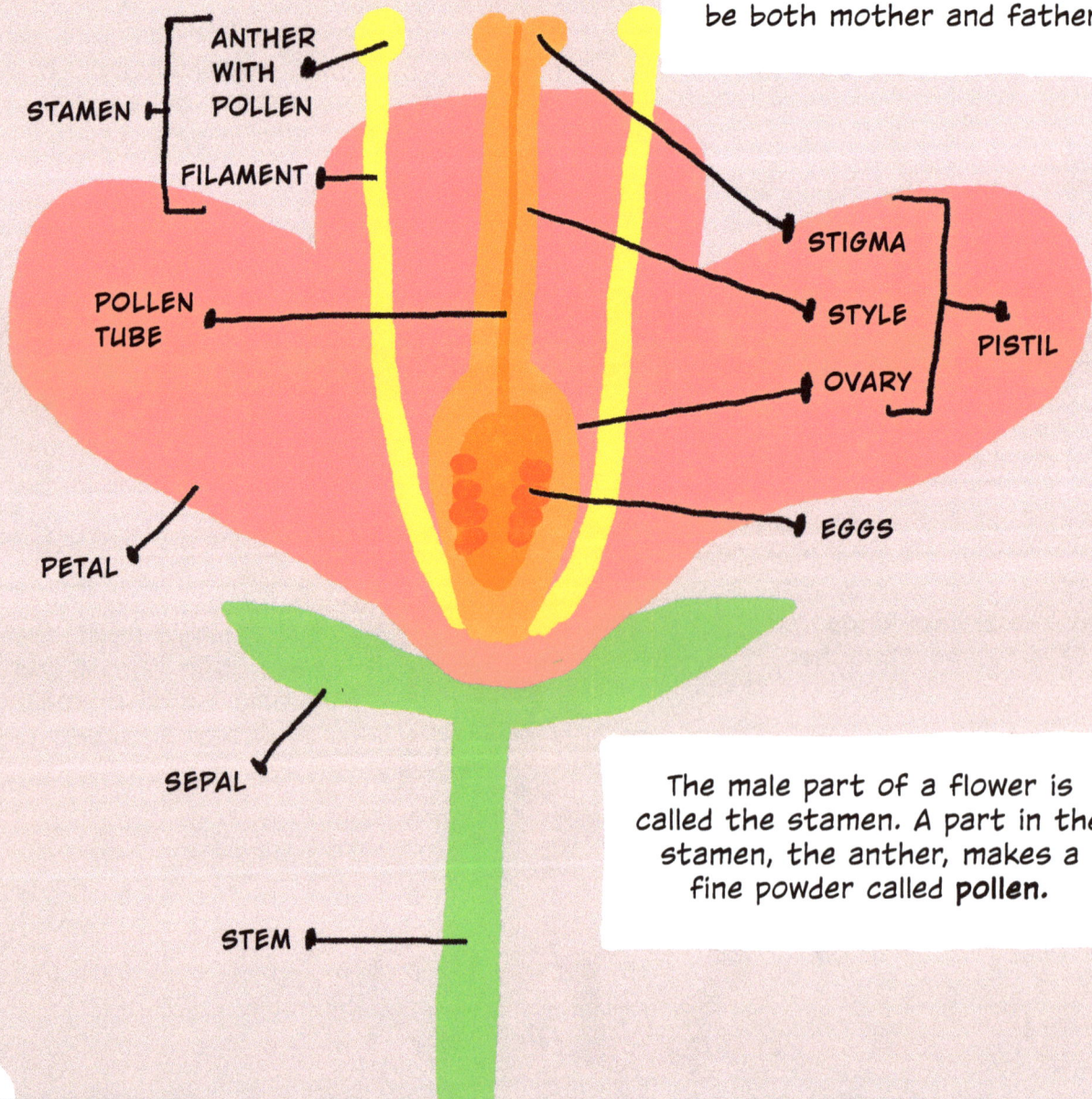

STAMEN

ANTHER WITH POLLEN

FILAMENT

POLLEN TUBE

STIGMA

STYLE

OVARY

PISTIL

EGGS

PETAL

SEPAL

The male part of a flower is called the stamen. A part in the stamen, the anther, makes a fine powder called **pollen.**

STEM

8

The female part, the pistil, contains the ovary.

STIGMA

STYLE

PISTIL

OVARY

EGG

The ovary is a structure within the flower body where a seed develops.

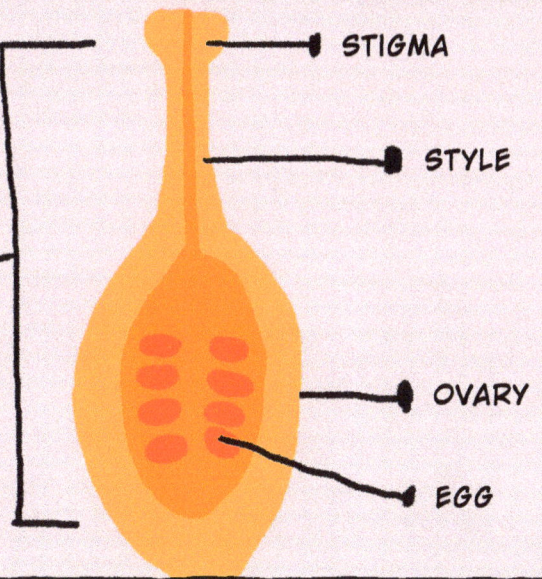

But a seed cannot develop on its own.

BBZZ

First, a single particle of pollen must deliver **sperm** cells to the ovary in a process called—

—pollination.

Once inside the ovary, the sperm can fertilize an **egg** and together—

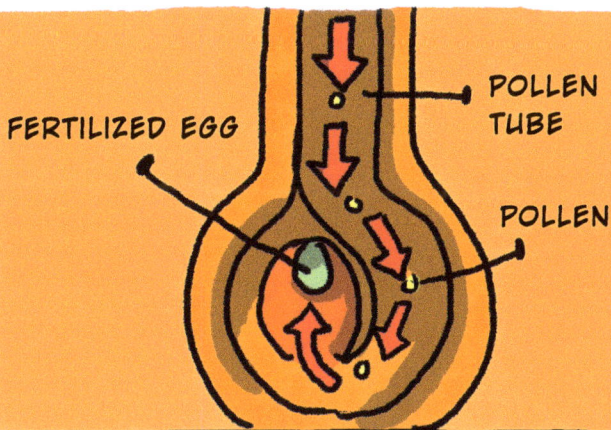

FERTILIZED EGG

POLLEN TUBE

POLLEN

—develop into a new seed!

Flowers can be so small that they are hard to see.

Other flowers are large and showy.

How can flowering plants have such variety?

Cross-pollination!

Plants can't move, so they need someone or something to move their pollen for them.

In fact, pollen can travel long distances away from its original location.

One way that a flower can promote cross-pollination is to produce a sweet fluid called **nectar.**

Nectar attracts bees, butterflies, birds, and other animals that drink the nectar for food.

While the animal visits the flower to drink the nectar, it becomes covered in pollen.

glug glug

Then, the animal carries the pollen to the next flower it visits.

If the pollen from one flower is transferred to the pistil of a flower on another kind of plant...

PISTIL

POLLEN

...cross-pollination has occurred.

That's how so many varieties of plants form!

Seeds come in many different shapes and sizes and are developed either inside or outside of the plant.

Seeds

enclosed   naked

Scientists divide seeds into two main groups, **enclosed seeds** and **naked seeds.**

Flowering plants produce enclosed seeds.

When an egg is **fertilized,** flowering plants produce enclosed seeds in the ovary.

The ovary serves as protection for the developing seed.

ENCLOSED SEED

In some plants, the ovaries develop into sweet, fleshy fruits you can eat, such as apples...

...peaches...

...and oranges.

Other plants, like peas and poppies, have dry fruits that form pods or capsules.

Grain plants, such as corn and wheat, form a hard kernel.

POP

Fruits are a way that plants can move their seeds around.

Plop

13

CONIFERS

Seeds produced on a nonflowering plant are called naked seeds.

A **conifer** is a seed plant that has no fruit or flowers.

Plants like this are also called **gymnosperms.**

Plop

Instead of enclosed seeds, conifer plants and other gymnosperms produce naked seeds.

Conifers include pine, fir, and many other evergreen trees.

These seeds are not protected within the plant during development.

On a conifer plant, seeds are made on the surface of structures called **cones.**

Conifers produce both male and female cones.

MALE

FEMALE

Male cones release a large amount of pollen that is carried away by the wind.

Female cones are larger and are usually higher up on the plant.

They make a sticky fluid that catches pollen.

plip
plip

If an egg on a female cone becomes fertilized by pollen, it develops into a naked seed.

Plop plop.

THE TRAVELING SEED

Different seeds have different features that help spread plants to new places.

The wind can carry seeds great distances, including the winglike seeds of the maple tree and the fluffy seeds of the dandelion plant.

3...
plop

These features can act like sails, and the seed can drift along a breeze to a new place.

Some seeds, such as those of the coconut, may float from one area to another—

Even reaching distant lands!

Animals also help distribute seeds.

Some plants have burs and sticky substances that attach seeds to the animal's fur. The seeds then fall off in a new place.

Many animals, such as birds and monkeys, eat the fleshy fruit from a flowering plant, but do not digest the seeds.

munch munch

The seeds pass out of the body as solid waste and fall to the ground in a new spot.

PLOP

Humans also help seeds travel, both by accident and on purpose, for example by spitting watermelon seeds.

PPT
PPT

A gardener moves seeds to a new place and grows plants to produce food.

Plop

Garden

Whenever a seed or seedling is planted in a new area, that new environment will affect the plant's growth.

The plant can also have an effect on other organisms in its new environment.

GERMINATION

When seeds reach the right location, they are triggered to grow, and **germination** can occur.

Germination is the development of a seed into a new plant and will start when conditions can help its growth.

These conditions may include water, sunlight, and warmth.

Seeds, such as bean seeds, can wait for months or even years to germinate and grow.

The tough outer coating that surrounds and protects a seed is called a seed coat.

Inside is a tiny plant called an **embryo** and tiny structures called cotyledons that store food.

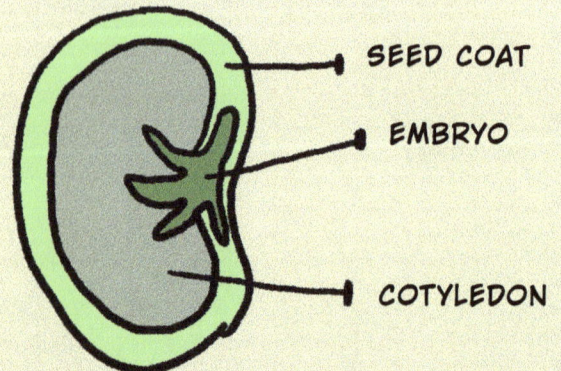

SEED COAT

EMBRYO

COTYLEDON

When the time is right, this bean seed coat splits open.

crack

crack

Then, a root pushes through the crack and grows into the ground.

pop

pop

A tiny stem pushes the cotyledon upward toward the sun.

pop

The developing plant can then make its own food through photosynthesis.

After a few leaves grow on the stem, the cotyledons fall away, and the seedling keeps growing into an adult plant.

Although each adult plant develops different parts, all seed plants begin with germination.

ASEXUAL REPRODUCTION

Another kind of reproduction, called **asexual reproduction,** involves only one parent.

The parent might be a single cell that makes two offspring.

The most basic kind of asexual reproduction is called **division.**

In division, a single cell splits to form two cells.

POP

Each of these cells is identical to the parent.

An offspring may also develop from part of a parent that grows or breaks off.

If part of the plant gets separated or falls off, it can grow into a whole new plant.

This kind of asexual reproduction is called **vegetative propagation.**

Vegetative propagation is common in leafy ground plants, such as the strawberry plant.

ROOTS

It grows stems along the ground called runners.

RUNNER

If a runner touches the ground, it may grow new roots, leaves, and stems, and become a new plant.

NEW ROOTS

SEEDLESS PLANTS

Some plants can go through both an asexual stage and a sexual stage of reproduction.

This kind of life cycle, the process of switching between asexual and sexual reproduction, is called the **alternation of generations**.

Consider the life cycle of a fern.

Unlike most plants, ferns do not make seeds.

Instead, they make **spores**.

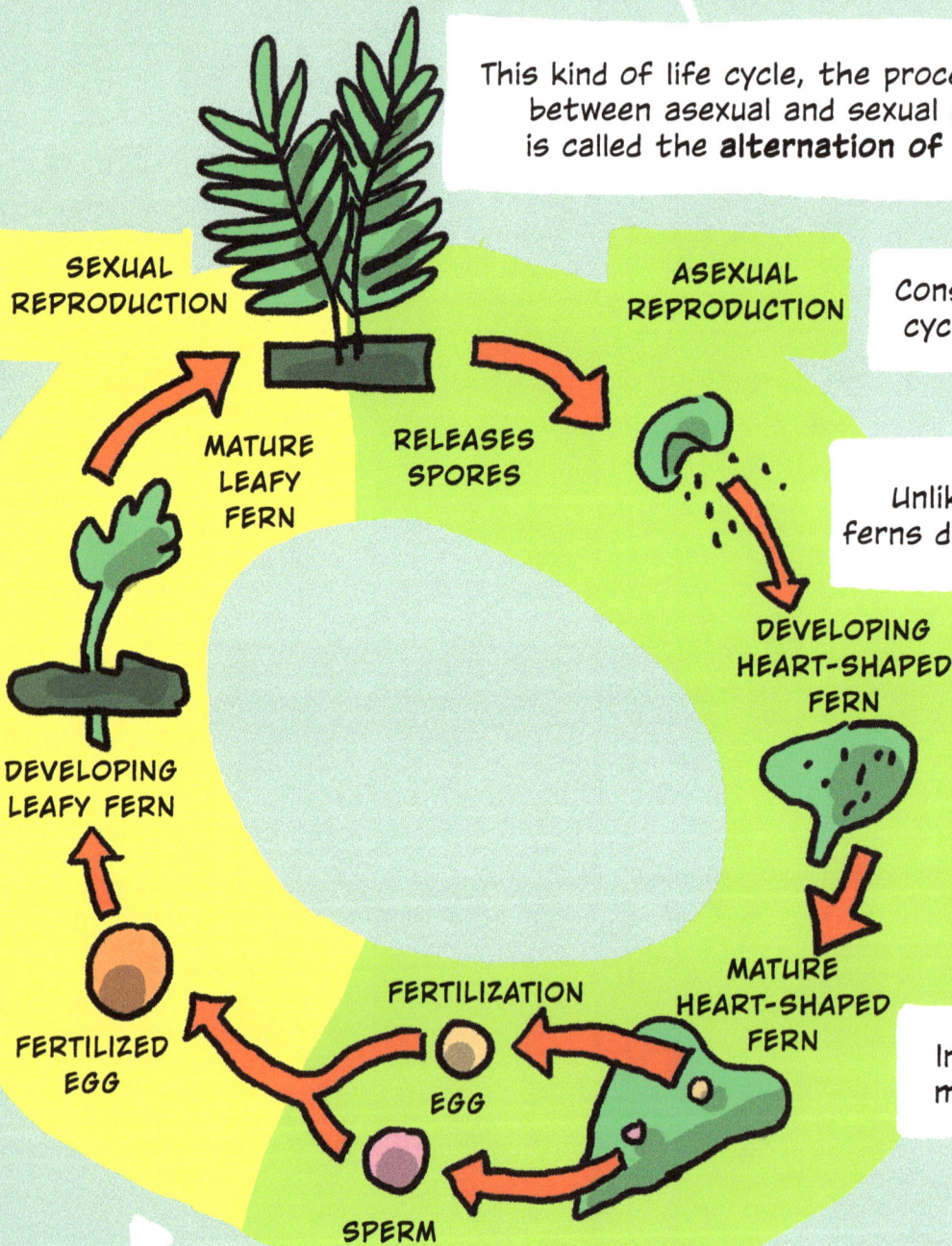

SEXUAL REPRODUCTION

ASEXUAL REPRODUCTION

MATURE LEAFY FERN

RELEASES SPORES

DEVELOPING HEART-SHAPED FERN

DEVELOPING LEAFY FERN

MATURE HEART-SHAPED FERN

FERTILIZED EGG

FERTILIZATION

EGG

SPERM

A spore is a tiny single cell that can grow into a new plant.

A leafy fern plant reproduces asexually by releasing spores.

These spores grow into a small, heart-shaped fern plant.

The new heart-shaped fern hardly resembles a leafy fern.

But when the heart-shaped fern begins sexual reproduction...

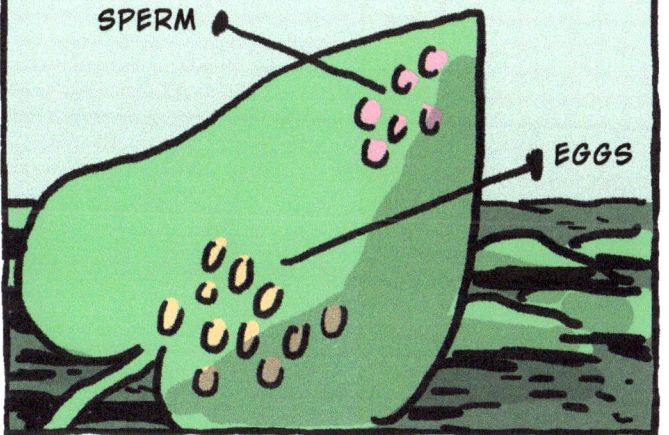

SPERM

EGGS

...the plant makes sperm and eggs.

SPERM

EGG

And if an egg becomes fertilized by sperm, it grows into a leafy fern.

GROWTH IN DIFFERENT CLIMATES

No matter its type of reproduction, the environment that a plant lives in has many impacts on its growth, development, and **life span**.

Plants can grow in many climates, but they have to adapt to their surroundings to be successful.

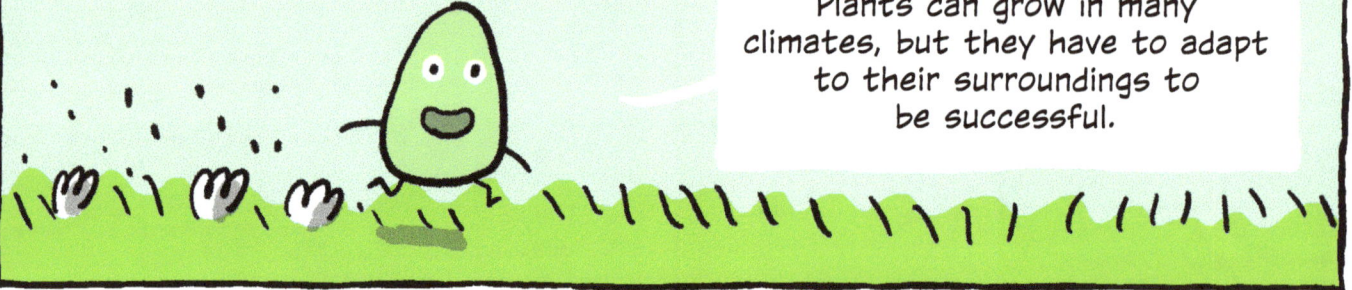

Most desert plants grow widely scattered from one another, lowering competition for water.

wipe

Some have extensive roots, allowing them to get water from large areas.

Some plants have a thick stem with waxy skin that holds water.

Other plants have short life spans due to rare rainfalls.

About 45 percent of the world's plant **species** occur in tropical rain forests.

In small areas of Asian and South American rain forests, scientists have counted over 250 species of trees!

Rain forests also support bamboos, herbs, shrubs, climbing vines, ferns, mosses, and flowers!

The diversity is, in part, due to favorable growing conditions, like massive amounts of rainfall and a tropical climate.

Because of continual moisture and warmth, tropical rain forests stay green all year.

Rain forests also provide shelter to many different animals.

These animals can help move seeds that grow into new plants.

As you can see, the location where a plant grows has a lot to do with its life cycle!

LIFE CYCLE DISRUPTIONS

A plant's life span is how long a plant can usually live in the wild.

Some plants have longer life spans than others.

Adult coast redwood trees typically grow 200 to 300 feet (60 to 90 meters) tall, and some can live more than 2,000 years.

A carrot has a shorter life span, growing from seed to mature plant in about 100 days.

Orange Juice

Many factors can lengthen or shorten a plant's life span.

Disruptions in plant life cycles can be caused by food shortages, lack of water, unfavorable growing conditions, diseases, pollution, invading species, and parasites.

Deforestation is a **life cycle disruption** caused by humans.

Logging trees to make room for farmland, new homes, or anything else...

...cuts short the life cycles of the other plants and animals living in that environment.

Forest fires can disrupt plant life cycles, but they can also aid in some plants' reproduction.

The heat from a raging fire can cause the scales on some conifer cones to open.

Seeds that survive the fire can fall into the freshly burned, nutrient-rich soil.

Over time, a new forest can grow from the ashes, and the cycle repeats itself.

27

Plants play an important part in your life cycle, too.

Your dependence on oxygen alone reveals just how important plants are to your life cycle.

And, whether a flowering plant, a naked seed, or a lone spore on a forest floor, all individual life cycles eventually come to an end. At the same time, new ones are just beginning!

POP POP POP POP POP

Woo-hoo!

Fossils of plants that died millions of years ago show that many different plants have been around for a very long time.

rattle

Yesss!

Thanks to reproduction and the alternation of generations, plants will continue to grow and change on Earth in the near future.

whiptch

Toss the fossil!

Your understanding of plants can grow and change along with all the life cycles around you.

swoop

My hat!

Run!

Just try planting a seed, and see what else you can learn about the plants around you!

vvroom

GLOSSARY

alternation of generations a type of life cycle in which a plant moves through both asexual and sexual reproduction.

angiosperm a flowering plant.

asexual reproduction the process by which an organism produces an offspring without sperm or egg cells.

cone part of a conifer plant that produces seeds.

conifer a type of plant that produces cones.

cross-pollination the process of carrying pollen from the anther of one plant to the pistil of another kind of plant.

division a kind of asexual reproduction where a single cell splits into two cells.

egg the female reproductive cell.

embryo a organism in the early stages of its development, just after fertilization.

enclosed seeds a kind of seed produced by angiosperms within the structure of the plant.

fertilize the process by which a male sperm cell and a female egg cell join together.

germination the process through which a seed sprouts and a plant begins to grow.

gymnosperm a nonflowering plant.

life cycle the stages that a living thing goes through as it develops.

life cycle disruption an unexpected shortening of an organism's life span.

life history the sequence of changes through which an organism passes during its lifetime.

life span the measure of how long an organism can live in the wild.

naked seeds a kind of seed produced by gymnosperms outside of the structure of the plant.

offspring the young of an organism.

organism any living thing.

photosynthesis the process by which plants make their own food.

pollen a fine, yellowish powder formed in the anther of a flower that fertilizes a plant's egg.

pollination the process of carrying pollen from the anther to the pistil of the same kind of plant.

reproduction the way living things make more of their own kind.

seedling a young plant.

sexual reproduction the process by which organisms produce offspring with sperm cells and egg cells.

species a group of closely related living things with many similarities.

sperm the male reproductive cell.

spore a single cell that can grow into a new plant.

vegetative propagation a form of asexual reproduction in plants.

FIND OUT MORE

Books

Backyard Biology: Investigate Habitats Outside Your Door with 25 Projects
by Donna Latham and Beth Hetland
(Nomad Press, 2013)

Ocean Sunlight: How Tiny Plants Feed the Seas
by Molly Bang and Penny Chisholm
(Blue Sky Press, 2012)

Photosynthesis
by Christine Zuchora-Walske
(ABDO, 2014)

Plant Parts
by Louise Spilsbury and Richard Spilsbury
(Heinemann, 2008)

Planting the Wild Garden
by Kathryn O. Galbraith and
Wendy A. Halperin
(Peachtree, 2011)

Plants: Flowering Plants, Ferns, Mosses, and Other Plants
by Shar Levine and Leslie Johnstone
(Crabtree, 2010)

The Secret Lives of Plants!
by Janet Slingerland and
Oksana Kemarskaya
(Capstone, 2012)

Websites

BBC Bitesize Science: Plant Life Cycles
http://www.bbc.co.uk/bitesize/ks2
/science/living_things/plant_life
_cycles/play/
Become a M.I. High Agent as you help
stop the spread of a dangerous plant
in this interactive game.

BBC Class Clips: An Introduction to Seed Germination and Growth
http://www.bbc.co.uk/learningzone/clips
/seeds/63.html
Track the full life cycle of a flowering
plant—from a small seed to mature adult!

BBC Nature: Animal and Plant Adaptations and Behaviours
http://www.bbc.co.uk/nature/adaptations
Life cycles are examined in short units,
complete with topic introductions and
wildlife video examples.

Missouri Botanical Garden: Biology of Plants
http://www.mbgnet.net/bioplants
/main.html
Make your way through this comprehen-
sive lesson to learn about plant structures, seeds, photosynthesis, and more!

National Geographic Kids – Green: Plants
http://video.nationalgeographic.com/video
/kids/green-kids/plants-kids/
Discover why plants are so important
to life on Earth as you watch this brief
nature video.

Nova: Illuminating Photosynthesis
http://www.pbs.org/wgbh/nova/nature
/photosynthesis.html
Learn more about photosynthesis as you
move step-by-step through the process
plants use to convert energy from the
sun into food.

Science Learning Hub: Plant Pollination
http://www.sciencelearn.org.nz/Contexts
/Pollination/Sci-Media/Video/Plant
-pollination
Listen to a narrated video describing how
plants use two strategies for pollination.

Scholastic Teachers: Science Study Jams!
http://studyjams.scholastic.com
/studyjams/jams/science/index.htm
All of your questions about plant and animal life will be answered in clickable les-
sons featuring narrated slideshows, key
terms, and short quizzes.

INDEX

alternation of generations, 22–23, 29
angiosperms, 8, 12, 28
animals, 7, 25
    pollination by, 10–11
    seed spreading by, 16–17, 25
anthers, 8

carbon dioxide, 5
cell division, 20
cells, 5, 7, 20, 22
cones, 15
conifers, 14–15, 27
cotyledons, 18, 19
cross-pollination, 10–11

deforestation, 26–27
desert plants, 24

eggs, 8, 9, 19, 22, 23
embryos, 18
enclosed seeds, 12

ferns, 22–23
fertilization, 12, 15, 22–23
flowering plants. *See* angiosperms
flowers, 8–9, 14
    pollination of, 10–11
forest fires, 27
forests
    destruction of, 26–27
    tropical rain, 25
fossils, 29
fruits, 13, 14, 17

germination, 18–19
global warming, 27
grain plants, 13
growth, 24–25
gymnosperms, 14

human beings, and plants, 26–27

life cycles. *See* plant life cycles
life spans, 24, 26

naked seeds, 12, 14–15, 28
nectar, 10–11

ovaries, 9, 12–13
oxygen, 5, 28

photosynthesis, 5, 19
pistils, 9
plant life cycles, 4–5
    and human life cycles, 28–29
    disruptions of, 26–27
pods, 13
pollen, 8, 15, 16
    See also pollination
pollination, 9
    cross-, 10–11

rain forests, 25
reproduction, 6–7, 29
    asexual, 20–23
    sexual, 7, 22–23
roots, 19, 21, 24
runners, 21

seed coats, 18–19
seedlings, 4, 17
seeds, 4, 6, 22, 27, 29
    conifer, 14–15
    development of, 9
    germination of, 18–19
    spreading of, 16–17
    types of, 12–13
spores, 22–23, 28
stamens, 8, 11
stems, 19, 21, 24

tropical rain forests, 25

vegetative propagation, 21

www.ingramcontent.com/pod-product-compliance
Lightning Source LLC
LaVergne TN
LVHW070840080426
835513LV00023B/2418